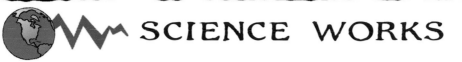 

SCIENCE WORKS

CHARGED UP
THE STORY OF ELECTRICITY

THIS WILL
BRIGHTEN UP
MY DAY.

Jacqui Bailey Matthew Lilly

Picture Window Books • Minneapolis, Minnesota

First American edition published in 2004 by
Picture Window Books
5115 Excelsior Boulevard
Suite 232
Minneapolis, MN 55416
1-877-845-8392
www.picturewindowbooks.com

First published in Great Britain by
A & C Black Publishers Limited
37 Soho Square, London W1D 3QZ
Copyright © Two's Company 2003

Printed in the United States of America.

Library of Congress Cataloging-in-Publication Data
Bailey, Jacqui.
Charged up : the story of electricity / written by
Jacqui Bailey ; illustrated by Matthew Lilly.— 1st American ed.
p. cm. — (Science works)
Summary: Describes how electrical energy is generated in
power stations and how it travels through pylons, power
cables, and wires into people's homes.
Includes bibliographical references and index.
ISBN 1-4048-0568-0 (Reinforced lib. bdg.)
1. Electricity—Juvenile literature. [1. Electricity.]
I. Lilly, Matthew, ill. II. Title.
QC527.2 .B28 2004
333.793'2—dc22   2003020116

For Louis
JB

For Phil and Alex
ML

4

Special thanks to our advisers for their expertise:

Paul Ohmann, Ph.D., Assistant Professor of Physics
University of St. Thomas, St. Paul, Minnesota

Susan Kesselring, M.A., Literacy Educator
Rosemount-Apple Valley-Eagan (Minnesota) School District

It was a bright sunny morning, but the weather forecast said there was a storm on the way.

Thick gray clouds rolled into view, and by noon there wasn't a patch of blue to be seen.

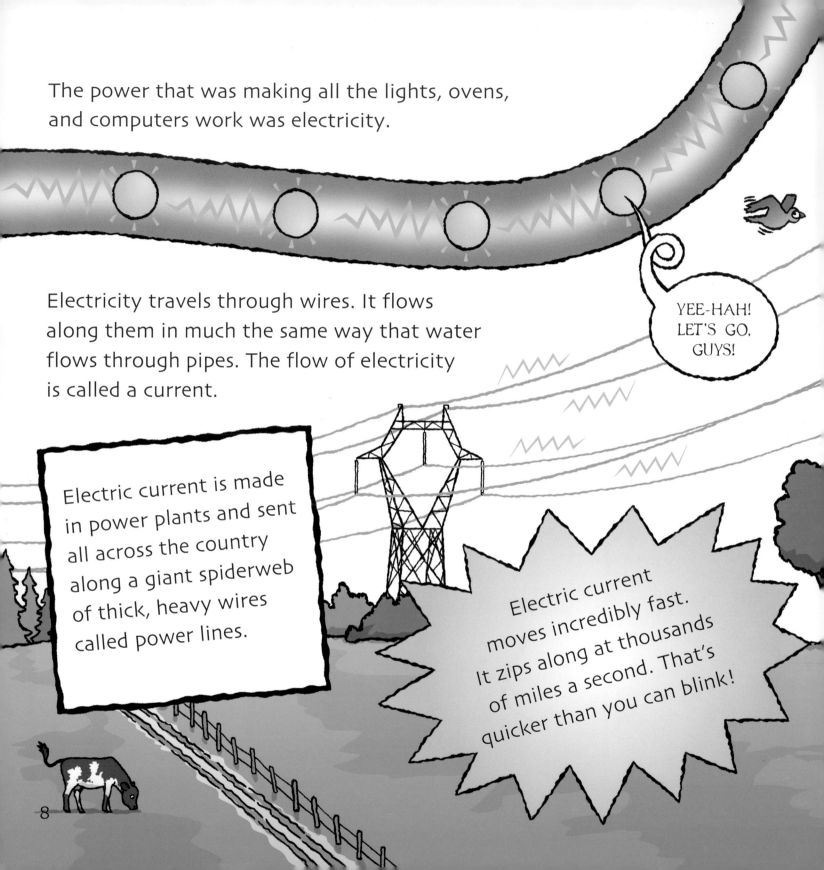

The power that was making all the lights, ovens, and computers work was electricity.

Electricity travels through wires. It flows along them in much the same way that water flows through pipes. The flow of electricity is called a current.

Electric current is made in power plants and sent all across the country along a giant spiderweb of thick, heavy wires called power lines.

YEE-HAH! LET'S GO, GUYS!

Electric current moves incredibly fast. It zips along at thousands of miles a second. That's quicker than you can blink!

Power plants turn one kind of energy (or power) into another. Most of the power the town used came from a hydroelectric (*hye-droh-i-LEK-trik*) power plant. It turned the energy of falling water into electricity.

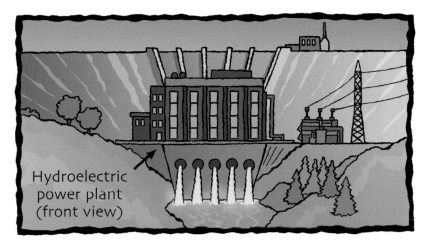

Hydroelectric power plant (front view)

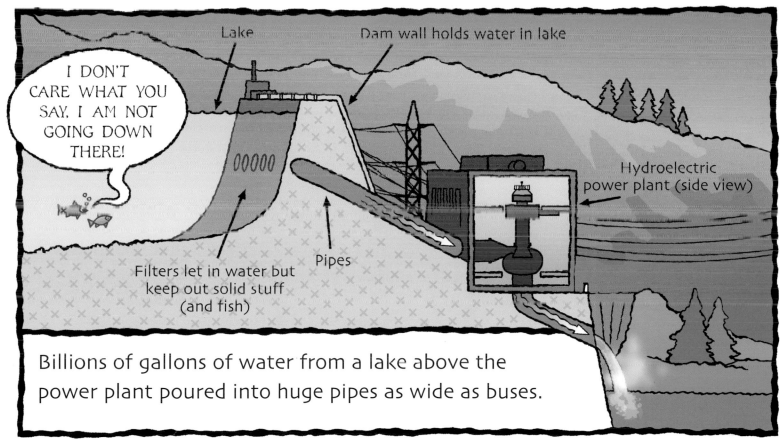

Lake

Dam wall holds water in lake

I DON'T CARE WHAT YOU SAY, I AM NOT GOING DOWN THERE!

Hydroelectric power plant (side view)

Filters let in water but keep out solid stuff (and fish)

Pipes

Billions of gallons of water from a lake above the power plant poured into huge pipes as wide as buses.

The pipes led to a row of machines called turbines inside the power plant. The turbines were like fat metal wheels, divided into sections by metal blades.

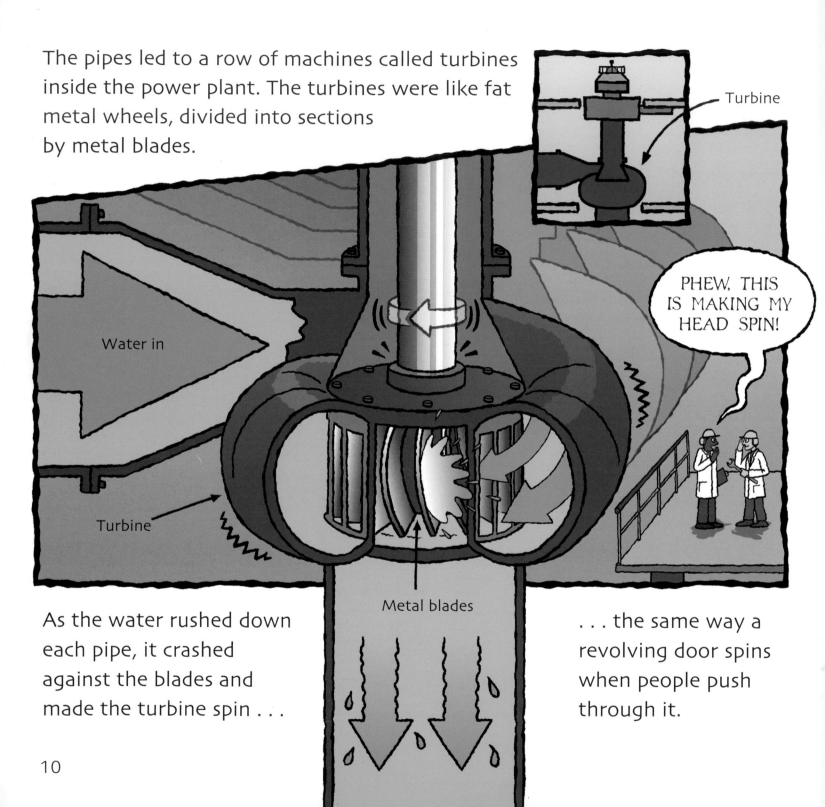

As the water rushed down each pipe, it crashed against the blades and made the turbine spin . . .

. . . the same way a revolving door spins when people push through it.

Turbine

Water out

The water raced around the turbine and out the other side into a river, which tumbled away down the hillside.

The water's job was done. All it had to do was make the turbine spin.

SEE, I TOLD YOU IT WAS A WATERFALL MACHINE.

As it spun, the turbine turned another wheel inside a machine called a generator.

The generator wheel was made of magnets, and magnets give out a special force called magnetism.

When the magnets whirled around, their magnetism made an electric current move inside some metal bands.

The current flashed from the metal bands into wires, which took it out of the power plant . . .

. . . and into a transformer.

The transformer's job was to give the current a boost so it could travel farther along the power lines. Otherwise, it would gradually lose some of its strength and stop flowing.

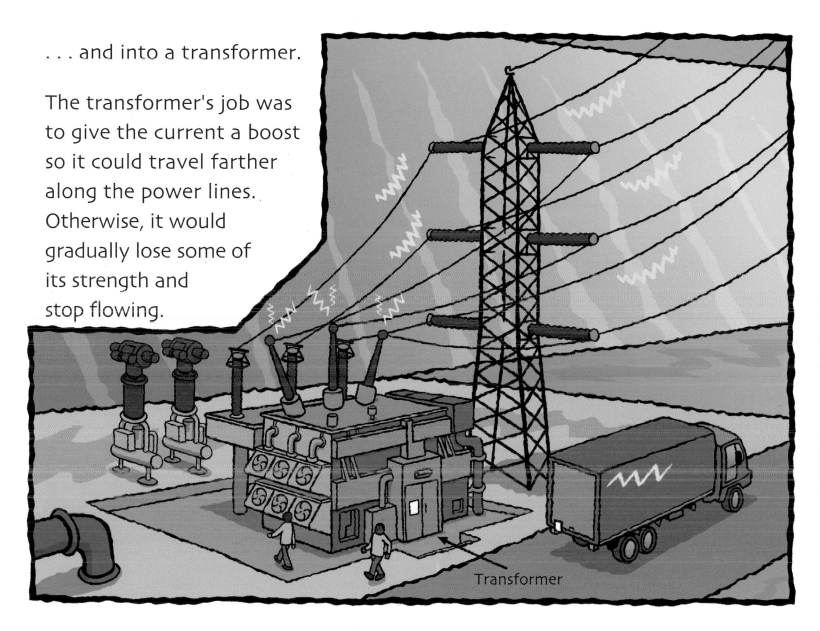

Transformer

The current raced out of the transformer and into the power lines. These were lifted high above the ground on giant metal towers called pylons. The pylons carried the lines away from the power station and across the countryside.

Meanwhile, high up in the sky the storm clouds billowed and tumbled.

Fat drops of rain splashed down, but the clouds weren't only stuffed with raindrops. They had millions of ice crystals in them, too.

WATCH OUT!

OUCH!

OOOF!

Inside the tumbling clouds, the ice crystals bumped and pushed against each other. As they bounced around, they began to build up energy.

The lightning headed for the ground, but it didn't get there. Instead, it hit a power line.

EEEEKK!

The power line was carrying current toward the town. When the lightning hit it, everything came to a stop!

HEY, I WAS WINNING. TURN IT BACK ON!

Lights went out. Televisions and radios died. Ovens stopped cooking, and computer screens went blank.

It was as if someone had thrown a gigantic blanket over everything. It was a power failure!

Far away, at the control center, an alarm flashed on a computer screen.

The alarm told the technicians there was a problem with one of the power lines. The technicians guessed the storm was to blame.

They knew they had to get electricity back to the people in the town as quickly as possible.

A team of technicians headed out to inspect the line.

The technicians knew the lightning must have sent a huge jolt of extra electricity into the power line. This extra jolt of electricity had set off the alarm, and safety switches at each end of the line had automatically turned the current off.

Before the current could be switched back on again, the technicians had to make sure the line wasn't damaged.

Luckily, the line was okay. The switches were turned back on, and current whizzed along it again.

Everything was back to normal. The current flowed along the power lines until it reached the edge of the town. Then it was fed into another transformer. This transformer made the current weaker so it was safe for people to use.

The current that travels along the power lines is so powerful, it would burn out most of the electrical machines we use.

Next, the current was split up and sent to different parts of the town. Some of it went into wires stretched between tall poles, and some of it went underground.

The poles carried the current away to a large factory on one side of the town . . .

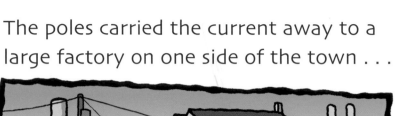

. . . and to a large farm on the other side.

THIS ONE IS A REAL LIVE WIRE!

The current that went underground traveled along thick cables beneath roads and sidewalks.

Some of the cables led to streetlights and traffic lights.

Others snaked off under paths, gates, and yards, into all of the offices, stores, and houses in the town.

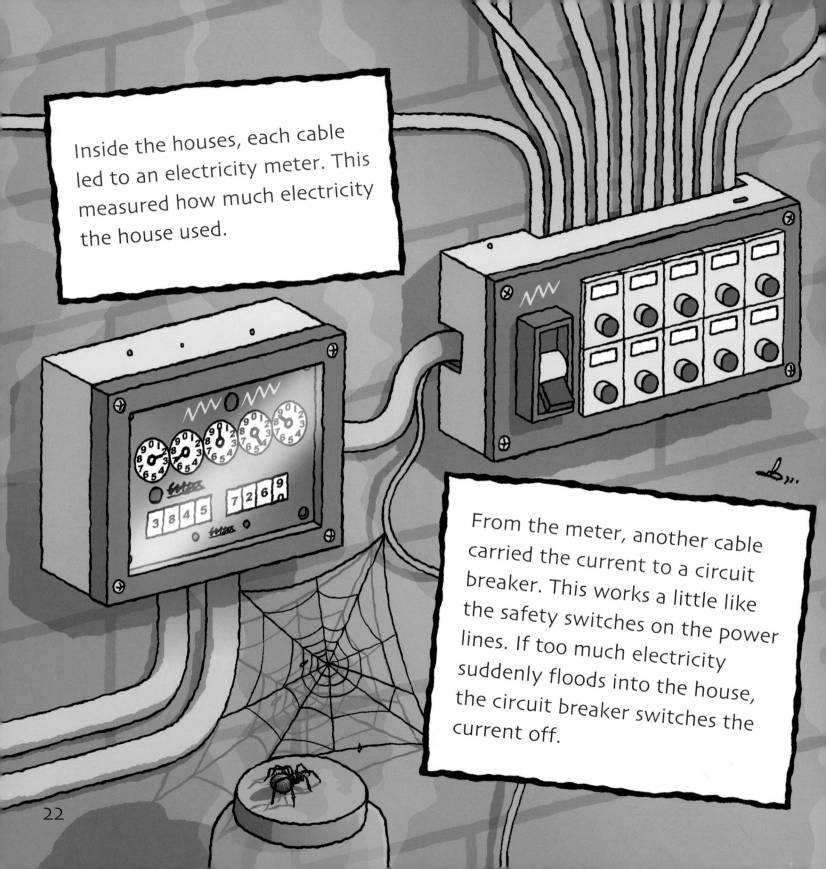

Inside the houses, each cable led to an electricity meter. This measured how much electricity the house used.

From the meter, another cable carried the current to a circuit breaker. This works a little like the safety switches on the power lines. If too much electricity suddenly floods into the house, the circuit breaker switches the current off.

From the circuit breaker, wires spread out all over the place.

They traveled under floorboards, inside walls, and across ceilings.

They led to light switches and lightbulbs and plugs.

The plugs led to heaters and hair dryers . . .

. . . toasters and televisions . . .

. . . telephones, fridges, and washing machines . . .

. . . and all of the things we use every day because we have electricity!

So the next time you reach over to turn on a switch, just think. Your switch is connecting you to . . .

1 Power plant makes electric current

2 Current is made stronger by transformer

3 Current flows along power lines carried on pylons

4 Transformer near town makes current weaker and splits it up

5 Some current goes into underground cables

6 Some current goes into wires carried by poles

7 Poles carry current to farm

24

8 Poles carry current to factory

9 Underground cables carry current to town

. . . thousands of feet of wires, and hundreds of pylons, machines, and people. It's bringing electricity all the way from the power plant to light your bedside lamp . . .

. . . all in the time that it takes to say, "Click!"

MORE GREAT STUFF TO KNOW

STEAMING ALONG

Hydroelectric power plants can only be built where water from mountain lakes and rivers can be made to fall from one level to another. Other power plants burn coal, oil, or gas fuels to heat up water to make a high-pressure steam. Then the steam is used to turn the power station's turbines.

Fuel-burning power plants work well, but the smoke they make causes pollution, and one day these fuels will run out. Scientists and engineers are looking for other ways of powering electricity turbines, such as using the energy from windmills.

BOXES OF ENERGY

I HOPE OUR BATTERY DOESN'T RUN OUT.

Not all electricity is carried along power lines. Some of it comes from batteries. Batteries have chemicals inside them that make small amounts of electricity. When the chemicals are used up, the battery stops working.

Batteries power all sorts of things from flashlights to toys and watches. They start the engine in a car and power its lights and heater. They are even used in submarines and spacecraft.

STATIC POWER

People make electric current travel along wires, but static electricity happens naturally all around us.

Static electricity makes your hair stand on end when you pull off a wool hat. It also makes lightning. When too much static electricity builds up inside a cloud, it looks for a way to escape. Lightning is electricity bursting out of the cloud!

Lightning often hits the highest thing within its reach. The safest place to be when lightning is around is indoors!

WOW, THIS STATIC IS HAIR RAISING STUFF.

WHAT A SHOCKER!

I FEEL SO STUNNING TODAY!

We aren't the only ones to make electricity. Some fish do it, too! Electric fish have special muscles that work like generators. The fish use their electricity to shock enemies or to stun or kill other animals for food.

The fish that gives the biggest shock is the electric eel. It lives in South American rivers and can grow as long as a ladder.

TRY IT AND SEE

LOOPING THE LOOP

Electric current has to flow around in a complete loop, called a circuit. If there is a gap or break in the circuit, the current will stop flowing.

Current flows through some materials more easily than others. Things that carry current well are called conductors. Things that don't are called insulators.

Try this experiment to see how a circuit works, and find out which materials make good conductors and which don't.

You will need:
- some thin, plastic-coated wire
- a 1.5-volt lightbulb and bulb holder
- a new 1.5-volt (type D) battery
- sticky tape, scissors, small screwdriver
- a collection of small objects
- an adult to help you

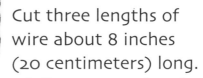

1 Cut three lengths of wire about 8 inches (20 centimeters) long. Next, carefully cut into the plastic coating about ½ inch (1 centimeter) from both ends of all three wires. Pull the plastic ends away, leaving a little bare wire.

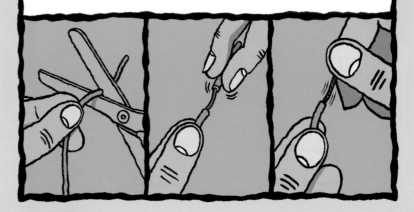

2 Take two pieces of wire, and hook one end of each piece around the screws on the bulb holder. Screw them down firmly. Then gently screw the bulb into the holder.

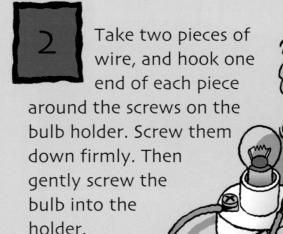

3 Tape the other end of one of the bulb wires to the bottom of the battery. Make sure the bare wire is touching the metal circle on the battery. Then take the third piece of wire and tape one end to the top of the battery.

4 You should now have all three pieces of wire connected to something but still have two loose ends—A and B.

End A

End B

Wire

Bulb

Wire

Battery

Bulb holder

Wire

5 Touch ends A and B together. This completes the circuit, and the bulb lights up. (If it doesn't, make sure your wires are firmly connected to the metal ends of the battery and the bulb holder.)

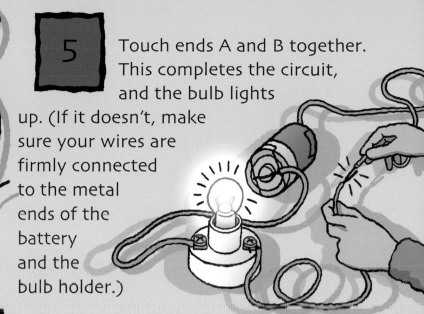

Try touching A and B to an object, such as a metal spoon. Both ends must touch the spoon. Does your bulb light up again? (Hint: Metal is a good conductor.)

Now try some other objects, such as a plastic spoon, a pencil, an empty glass, a pencil eraser, a key, and a wool glove. Which objects make the best conductors and which ones make the best insulators?

ELECTRIFYING FACTS

Your body has millions of tiny electrical messages zipping around it all the time. The messages travel along your nerves from your eyes, ears, mouth, skin, and muscles to your brain and back again. They even keep your heart beating.

A single bolt of lightning has enough energy in it to keep a lightbulb lit, day and night, for more than three months.

Power plants began making electricity in the 1880s. One of the first to open was in New York City in 1882. It was built by Thomas Edison, who also invented the first lightbulb in 1879.

INDEX

FACT HOUND

Fact Hound offers a safe, fun way to find Web sites related to this book. All of the sites on Fact Hound have been researched by our staff. *http://www.facthound.com*

1. Visit the Fact Hound home page.

2. Enter a search word related to this book, or type in this special code: 1404805680.

3. Click the FETCH IT button.

Your trusty Fact Hound will fetch the best sites for you!